Adventures in Arbitrage

One Man's Journey through the Jungle of
eBay to Prosperity on the Amazon River

JOHN GROLEAU

DEDICATION

This book is dedicated to my Lord and Savior Jesus Christ.
Through him, all things are possible.

I would also like to thank the following individuals:
Cynthia, my wife – for her unerring support
Chris Green – for his unselfish devotion to his craft and the book *Retail Arbitrage*
Adrianne Peri – for her friendship and mentoring. Without her I would be stuck on eBay.

CONTENTS

37	BOLOs and BOGOs	73
38	Future Thoughts	76
	Appendix 1 – 25 Quick Tips	80
	Appendix 2 – Business Analysis of First 18 Months	85
		86
	Appendix 3 – Recommended Reading	
		87
	Appendix 4 – Recommended Online Sources	

FOREWORD

I want to be absolutely up front and honest with you. This is not your typical book on how to sell on Amazon or eBay. There are numerous books on the subject -- see Appendix 3. Simply put, this is *my story*, my experience of more than 20 years of selling, first at flea markets, then graduating to eBay full-time, followed by my transition to Amazon in March of 2012. On that platform I achieved a successful $1 million in sales in my first 18 months.

It is my hope in writing this book to share my successes and failures over that 20 year period. In doing this, hopefully I can help others towards success in their own quest and possibly help them avoid some of the pitfalls I encountered. This book is not a how-to book, but just a yarn on how I did it. The good, the bad, and the ugly, as it were. Hopefully within these pages everyone can learn a little something. Maybe avoid a mistake, gain encouragement, or simply get ideas.

After reading this book, if you feel it was not worth the paper it was printed on or the digital space it took up, please feel free to request a refund and you will receive one -- no questions asked. Same guarantee I have offered on eBay for 19 years and on Amazon for the last two. :)

INTRODUCTION

My story actually started 20 years ago when I was stationed in Washington D.C. I was approaching 20 years of active duty in the United States Air Force. I had recently remarried and was expecting a new addition to our family. The expense of living in the Washington D.C. Metropolitan area was very high, and even as an E-7 there were financial difficulties. I have always been a student of the economy to a finite degree. It was very discouraging that although I loved serving my country, my family suffered because of what was (I thought at the time) low pay compared to my civilian counterparts. One never, ever fully knows another's circumstances, but it seemed everyone was more affluent than me. So I searched constantly for ways to improve my family's financial situation.

Weekends and nights were spent doing remodeling jobs for friends and fellow staff members of the AFIP (a medical research facility located on the campus of Walter Reed AMC) where I was stationed. I even went so far as to create my first business entity, "Miracle Builders. If I build it and it stays up, well it's a miracle!" As you can see, my sense of humor was even then my best quality during those trying times, and it served me well over the next couple of decades as I tried to find the entrepreneurial avenue that would bring me financial security.

During those first couple of years, I was exposed to yard sales by my new wife. I discovered that a person could go to yard sales and antique stores and buy items and resell them in your own booth at an antique mall or, even better yet, sell them at flea markets. It was thus that my sojourn into the crazy world of flea markets had begun. Little did I know at the time that this was the start of a journey that would take my family and I from Washington D.C. to the back woods of West Virginia and on to the beaches of Florida. There were times I was so poor I was homeless.

Through sheer luck and hard work I have now arrived at my present situation where I own my own condo, free and clear. I live across the street from the ocean in an idyllic setting and have a successful business selling on the Amazon river via fulfillment by Amazon FBA. And so the adventure begins....

Book One:

Heading into the Jungle
The Early Years

1 FLEA MARKETS

The good, the bad and the homegrown... Do I hear banjos being strummed?

Winchester, Virginia. The entrepreneurial adventure into arbitrage started at the Double Toll Gate Flea Market in this quaint city bordering West Virginia. My sister, Linda, had recently bought some land in Capon Bridge, West Virginia, and we would visit occasionally on weekends. While we were there, she would invite us to come visit her at her table at the flea market. She sold mainly antiques and toys and was making good money for the time, about $500 a weekend.

This really intrigued me as I was in full-fledged remodeling mode and busting my butt for about $200 a weekend. Laying tile, plumbing, painting, and remodeling in general is very hard physical labor, especially when meeting the stringent demands of a client. The concept of relaxing at a table at a flea market and doubling my money was very intriguing indeed. Little did I know then the pitfalls of such an endeavor....

Exaggeration versus the little white lie. We all do it. As humans we tend to exaggerate our situation, be it good or bad. What I thought was $500 income was $500 in sales. A big difference I soon learned.

Considering Winchester was almost a two hour drive from our home, gas was a major expense. Couple that with table rent, cost of goods, and storage fees for inventory, our actual profit was only around $150 a weekend. Depressingly less than I could make in the same amount of time remodeling.

However, it was fun. Flea market vendors are a strange and unique sampling of what humanity has to offer, present company excluded of course. ;)

It was at this flea market we met a married couple whose small child you would have sworn was E.T.'s little brother. The couple themselves was straight out of the "Lil Abner" comic strip. One had only two teeth, the other missing the exact same two teeth. I honestly believe they were Siamese twins separated at birth. They became my first introduction to selling used books, bringing a U-Haul truck full and setting up tables full of books in an octagon shape. The books were stored in these three-shelf boxes so when they placed them on the tables they would lean back at an angle.

It worked great, except you couldn't see the sellers to pay or ask a question, which on second thought was probably a pretty good idea. :)

Well, to make a long story short, they sold paperbacks for a quarter and hard cover books for a dollar, regardless of condition, value, or venue. This model became a valuable resource for sales and my first experience with replenishables. Through their help I was able to raise my net income to $300 a weekend, and remodeling was quickly disappearing from my resume.

Being a vendor at a flea market has its perks as well as pitfalls. The perks are the freedom of being your own boss, setting your price, and experiencing pure capitalism without government intervention. I seriously doubt 1 in 100, if that, ever reported income from their sales in those days. The concept of 'flipping' first occurred to me back then. While other vendors were intent on getting 'their price,' I saw the advantage of selling all of my inventory so I did not have to cart it all back to Arlington and pay storage fees. Many a weekend culminated with us selling our entire inventory to another dealer for a 'steal,' sometimes less than I had paid for the items.

However, I learned early on that if customers didn't buy it the first weekend, they were not going to buy it the next. I was quickly experiencing the phenomenon where the last thing I purchased was the first thing to sell, hmmm. As things developed, I soon found myself sourcing on the way to and even at the flea market.

One situation comes to mind where we parked the truck, leaving everything on it and heading for the yard sale section of the flea market. Most outdoor flea markets have a section for rent for 'non-professionals,' as we call them.

These are virtual Meccas of inventory from individuals outside the mainstream flea market seller. On this particular morning, the first yard-saler had a treasure trove of small toys. I dug in, quickly settling on two pieces from the McDonald's Happy Meal train set, specifically the Barbie and the truck with a gift box in the cargo area. The Barbie piece for the train had been recalled because you could pull the doll off the piece and that left a sharp pointy needle perfect for removing the eye of a small child. The truck on the other hand was a solid piece, but the gift box was small and easily lost or swallowed, so these were the HTF (hard to find) part of the set.

Also, to my surprise, there were several older toys in the batch, and what caught my eye was a die cut un-footed Mickey Mouse Pez dispenser. I gathered up my loot and approached the young mother of three. "Twenty-five cents each," she demanded. I gave her a dollar and smiled, telling her "keep the change." Similar finds were to be had from other sellers.

Exactly two hours later, the two McDonald's toys sold for $10 each, paying for my table rent for the whole weekend. By the end of the weekend, every item I bought that morning had sold, except for the Mickey Pez dispenser. That little treasure was with me for all of five days, when it brought $225 at a local auction. Not a bad return on a 50 cent investment.

What didn't sell? All of the items I carted up from D.C., several antiques, some furniture, and a ton of heavy Depression Glass. I had learned a valuable lesson. Buy what others like, not what I like.

2 THE BEANIE BABY PHENOMENON

As my retirement from the Air Force was pending, I started searching for a line of products that would sell anywhere, as I was contemplating retiring to Florida. I was still selling toys and other collectibles and doing quite well. But I was not sure how these would sell in Florida, and it was a long way to the huge antique malls of Pennsylvania to source. As luck would have it, I stopped by my sister's table prior to setting up one day and saw a table full of these little bean bag animals. When she explained to me these were TY Beanie Babies and the latest fad along with the McDonald's Happy Meal versions, I knew I had to have some.

"Where on earth did you find them?" I asked. My sister took me aside and said "You know the little pharmacy down the street? They have hundreds of them for $4.95 each, so don't set up yet -- go buy some." Taking it on faith, I drove the mile down the street, piled up a cart, whipped out a credit card, and bought 100 of the little buggers, mainly focusing on the bears, as she said they were quick sellers. Well, I sold them all by noon for $8 to $10 a piece and made three subsequent trips back to that pharmacy, as well as a couple of Hallmark stores, and had my first $1,000 net weekend. I was on my way!

To this day I still do not know why the customers didn't just drive the mile down the street -- was it ignorance or laziness? I have no idea, but I was more than happy to be the middle man.

There were several beanies that were already retired but still available. Being 'retired' meant you could charge $15 each versus the going rate of $8 on the secondary market. Also TY occasionally mis-tagged items and changed the names on several beanies, creating a higher demand and a subsequent rise in price. Learning which beanies were which and the prices of such was very important. Although I didn't sell beanies on eBay, it was a great price guide and put me ahead of the game with other vendors.

The majority of people selling at flea markets didn't know how to turn on a computer, never mind how to access the internet. Alas, all good things must come to an end. Now sellers at yard sales and flea markets alike quote current buy-it-now prices, which is complete misinformation, but that is another part of the story...

3 FLORIDA OR BUST

In February 1996 I made the big step and moved to Florida armed with all the vim and vigor of a 39-year-old retiree. I just knew the Sunshine State would welcome me with open arms. Such was not the case; instead I found a 'good ole boy network' that I was not the least bit prepared for. I sent my resume to 100 prospective employers and received three interviews and absolutely zero job offers. During this time we were selling a little on eBay and a little at the flea markets. I was trying everything I knew to make money. Beanies were still popular, but the word was out. There were a dozen sellers at each market, and the competition was fierce. We were suffering financially, so I decided to become a realtor; I was going to corner the real estate market.

In reality, what happened was I wrote more contracts than any other rookie in the history of the company. The problem was, I couldn't close. Out of nearly 100 contracts only seven went to fruition -- we were just not making it. My wife was making more money as a waitress than I was as a Real Estate Tycoon, so back to the fleas I went.

During the next few months, I was able to build my sales up to a respectable $1,000 a weekend, but my net from sales was only about $300, and the stress was building.

Once again fate intervened. My wife had met a couple of young men who lived between 3rd Street and the beach, right in the heart of local antique shops. They were going to have a yard sale in their front yard and invited us to put up a few tables and sell our beanies. To say it was successful was an understatement. I sold out the first day! All of the inventory we had, $3,000 net in one day! I had finally found my niche. Hello rich and famous! Boy was I ready. Over the summer I sold over $65,000 in TY Beanie Babies in their front yard. Life was good.

All good things must come to an end, and when the summer ended so did the crowds and the sales. Once again fate intervened when a young couple with a baby approached us on the last weekend of the summer. The young man stated that his mom had an antique mall in the small town of St. Mary's just across the border in Georgia. Both his wife and his mom loved Beanie Babies. Unfortunately, the only Hallmark store in town was sold out the same day each shipment arrived. We drove up the next day and secured a 36" wide book case in her mall for $15 monthly with no commission needed.

That weekend I filled the bookcase with 135 beanies and went home with our fingers crossed. Monday morning the proprietor of the mall called and asked when in the hell was I gonna get there and refill my case as she was tired of turning away customers. Once again I had struck gold, so we loaded up the Celica and moved to St. Mary's, the patron saint of Beanie Babies. :)

4 JERRY GARCIA, REST IN PEACE

A Purple Princess and a Dark Blue Elephant.

Early in the Beanie Baby phenomenon, TY came out with a tie-dye bear they called Garcia. It was one of many beanies TY ended up renaming because of alleged copyright infringements. This time the controversy was the bear was supposedly named after Jerry Garcia of the Grateful Dead. TY subsequently took the bear and sewed a peace symbol on its chest, renaming it Peace. The result of this was Garcia bears were now selling from $50 to $100 each, while Peace was a $15 bear. Other name changes included Doodles the rooster becoming Strut and Tabasco the pig becoming Snort. I mention these because they still are worth picking up versus common beanies.

In July of 1996 I attended and set up at the first ever Jacksonville Beanie Baby show at the Ramada Inn. I was cocky as hell, I was the man. I showed up prepared to sell out my vast inventory of over 1,500 beanie babies. Instead I got spanked. There were sellers from all over the country, even as far away as California. I was small potatoes compared to most of these sellers, and my sales for the day showed it. One seller had dozens of every retired beanie, even a few I had never seen before. It was daunting and a lesson learned.

One person did fare worse than me at the show. This individual purchased a dark blue peanut elephant for $7800, bragging it was going to put his son through medical school. Instead three years later this item would fetch a mere $500. Another lesson learned. I

11

did make a major score at this show, not in selling but in buying. The vendor next to me was a Hallmark dealer, and in violation of TY's policies she was selling on the secondary market.

She had boxes of Princess Di bears and Erin the Emerald Isles bears. These were the most highly anticipated new beanies ever. I stood by and watched as she sold dozens of these bears for $300 apiece. Her cost $2.50. During the show I helped her to set up and relieved her for potty breaks etc. I was in awe of the amount of money exchanging hands over pieces of material filled with small Styrofoam pellets.

As we approached the end of the show I negotiated with her to give me a deal at the end if she had any left. For brevity sake, when the smoke had cleared she had one unopened box from TY filled with 36 Princess Di bears. After much haggling we settled on a price of $85 each or $3,000 dollars. I arranged to meet her at her home, and Monday morning I was the proud owner of 36 TY Princess Di bears. To say that I was nervous was an understatement. What if they didn't sell? What if the stores became flooded with them?

This was by far the most I had ever paid for any inventory, beanie or otherwise and represented all of our savings. With a prayer on my lips I deposited the bears at my three selling locations. I set a price of $185 each and went home a nervous wreck. Within one hour of opening each store called me to report I was sold out. I had made $3,600 profit in one hour! Another lesson was learned: know your product and don't be afraid to pull the trigger.

5 A SHOT FIRED ACROSS THE BOW

This is a term I use to describe when warning signs are given by the heavens. In March of 1997 I was in full blown Beanie Baby retail mode. I had three outlets selling dozens a week. I myself was selling 100+ daily at a local flea market. My marriage was going well, and finally life was good. A highly anticipated TY beanie retirement was scheduled. TY had announced on their website that on March 31 they were going to retire several of their current line. Everyone in the business was excited. Dollar signs were in our eyes. The night before the announcement I made up a flyer for each location announcing the retirement.

Basically, no one knew which beanies were going to be retired, but a retired beanie immediately doubled in price. My standard price for currents was $8, and a common retiree was $15. In my flyer I graciously offered to sell whichever new retiree at the current price until 2:00 pm, at which time they would increase in price to at least $15 each. I went home with visions of $ signs jumping over fences as I finally fell asleep.

About 10:00 am my pager went haywire. All three locations were paging me. I sped out of my driveway with a grin on my face. When I approached my first retail outlet, a place called Whispers, I spotted a couple of police cars out front. In my naïveté I thought maybe they were there to escort me to the bank. I could not have been more wrong...

Apparently at 8:00 am when the small antique mall opened there were at least 40 patrons in line outside. Upon opening the door the owner was basically trampled by customers heading to my booth. When the smoke cleared, over 350 beanies were gone and only 27 had been purchased. Upon leaving Whispers and heading to Mike's comic shop, I received another urgent page, this time from Mike. When I arrived, I found the shop locked and a haggard Mike next door at the pawn shop.

Apparently, he too had been bombarded by ladies with large handbags, and as he rang one up he would notice several leaving without purchasing. After ten minutes at a frenetic pace, he realized what was happening and shut down his store. He was waiting for the police also. The same rang true for my third location. In a period of less than two hours, twenty or so women with large handbags stole over 700 Beanie Babies from my three retail outlets.

Was this an organized group or just a thieving frenzy? No one was ever caught nor were similar situations reported locally. There were some reports on the news of TY trucks being hijacked, warehouses broken into, and Hallmark stores robbed. Things were definitely getting out of hand. I decided to quit the Beanie Baby business, and over the next three months I sold off my inventory for $5 a beanie at three flea markets. As I was selling the last few pieces word was coming in that TY was flooding the market, and the Beanie Baby phenomenon was history. I had dodged the bullet and another lesson was learned.

6 JOHN, FIND A JOB!

After the Beanie Baby debacle my finances were once again hurting, and so was the marriage. I contacted my old job at AFIP and was offered a GS-13 administrator position. John was going back to working for the man... Not a pleasant thought. I packed up the family, moved to Virginia, interviewed for the position, and waited for Congress to approve the funding. We had set up household in a small apartment in a very depressed neighborhood while waiting for me to start the job. I wasn't concerned, as it was a temporary solution. However, Congress was dragging their feet on the budget and what was supposed to be weeks became months.

Because it was winter and the local fleas were not very productive, I spent more time going to yard sales and selling on eBay. We were barely getting by. I thought about returning to remodeling, but instead got the idea to build custom-made furniture. I went to the local Walmart to buy a couple of wood-working magazines to get some ideas. I remember I was shocked at the time that a few magazines would cost me almost $20, so I returned them to the shelf. That weekend I stopped at a church sale and found several stacks of WOOD magazines for $1 a stack -- jackpot -- so I bought them all for $10 (about 300 magazines). When I got them home, I put them in the closet and quickly forgot them, and any notion I had of building furniture slipped away.

7 JEFF GORDON, I OWE YOU ONE

Time dragged on. The budget was delayed again and again. I started applying for jobs elsewhere, to no avail. I was over-qualified. I was returning from an interview when I stopped to buy groceries. At the entrance there was this huge display of four-packs of Pepsi and Mountain Dew with Jeff Gordon's picture on them and car 24. I have never been a fan of Nascar, but heard at the time it was pretty collectible. Anyway, the four-packs were selling for $0.94 per four-pack. I figured what the heck, if they didn't sell we had soda for a decade, and bought the whole display. It was this type of behavior that led to the end of my marriage, but I didn't see it at the time.

Upon arriving back to my tiny apartment with a truck full of Pepsi and no job, sparks flew, which was becoming more and more the standard for our relationship. After defending my position, I sheepishly carried the first four-pack into the house and with bated breath typed "Jeff Gordon Pepsi 24" into the search bar on eBay. As the listings populated, it became evident the going price was $8 a bottle, and they were selling. I had dodged the bullet again. Apparently Pepsi Co was only releasing them in limited markets around the country, and as a result, Jeff Gordon kept my family fed and housed over that winter in Virginia. Thanks, Jeff.

8 CAPITAL ONE, MY TICKET TO SUNSHINE

As the dreary winter dragged on (oh, have I told you I hate winter?) no word was coming down on the government job. The market on Pepsi was flattening out, and the only job offer on the table was $12 an hour working for Capital One. This was barely enough to pay rent. I was really tired of the cold weather and the traffic in northern Virginia. I had nearly given up hope, when the recruiter for Capital One called and said they had openings for both myself and my wife at their call center in Tampa, Florida. Sunny Florida, I was elated. My hopes were soon dashed as no relocation assistance was offered, so we would have to move on our own dime. I still agreed, and we made plans to downsize our belongings to a U-Haul trailer.

As we discussed what we could get rid of and what not, I got another lesson in the difference between men and women. I could move with the clothes on my back. My wife insisted everything we had was a necessity. We were at an impasse once again. How many times am I going to hit the wall, I wondered?

9 WONDER WOMAN TO THE RESCUE

As I looked around the small apartment, I looked for items I could sell to finance the move. There just wasn't anything left of value. I sat down on the couch in complete despair. At that moment, "Wonder Woman" came on TV and threw her lasso around my brain. I suddenly remembered selling the first edition of MS magazine on eBay a few weeks earlier for $20. Wonder Woman was on the cover. Now, if I only had 100 copies of that magazine...but I didn't. All I had was several hundred copies of wood working magazines in the closet that I had to take to Goodwill tomorrow.

"Wait a minute," I thought, "if the first edition of MS is worth 20 bucks, maybe early editions of WOOD magazine are worth something." I hurried to my computer and typed in 'first wood magazine' ... Score! $60. Number 2, $40. Numbers 3 through 10, $20 each. Come to find out, that pile of magazines that I bought at that church sale would sell for almost $2,400. We had our moving money -- Sunshine State, here we come. One note: although the value of woodworking magazines has dropped, collectors do still want the early editions, and they are not available from the publisher. Over the next couple of years, I estimate I made another $5,000 on these types of magazines alone on eBay. :)

Working for Capital One was anything but fun. Being a call center customer service representative must be one of the most stressful jobs in America. Picture having a disgruntled card holder basically hollering at you for ten minutes, then at the end of the call you are required to sell them something. It goes something like this: "Mr. Smith, I apologize for my company screwing you like this. There is nothing I can do about it. Now, in appreciation of you as a customer, please let me sell you something else you don't need that is totally worthless." Get my drift? Almost every shift ended with going across the street for happy hour. The job sucked.

One Friday as I was driving to work, I saw a small preprinted sign on the side of the road. It said "Closeouts, new manufacturer rep items for sale" Huh? Since I was already late for work, I flipped a U-turn and went hunting. What I found was a garage full of boxes. In the boxes were hundreds of books and greeting cards. The books were comic strip books like *Calvin and Hobbes*, *The Far Side*, etc. The seller was a rep for the publisher Rand McNally, and these boxes represented overstock items and shelf-pulls when new items were delivered. They had been piling up in her garage for the last five years.

All of the books were brand new, and there were dozens of each title. The greeting cards were new also. They had pictures of children, dogs, cats, and other small animals on the cover. The insides were blank. The prices on the cards were $1.50 each, and the books ran from $14.95 to $19.95 each. She was asking $1 per book and only 10 cents per card. I had no idea what their value might be in resale but quickly bought one of every book and a dozen or so cards and rushed off to work.

I promptly forgot about them until Sunday afternoon when unloading my car from a weekend of yard-saling. Much to my surprise, I found the books more often than not were selling for more than the cover price. I should have thought of this, considering my success with magazines, but I honestly hadn't even considered it. I jumped back into my car and rushed to the lady's home. Much to my chagrin, the house was locked up tight as a drum, and there was a for-sale sign in the front yard. Not to be daunted, I called the realtor and asked about the location of the seller. Apparently the seller was still in Tampa, and after a brief phone conversation I learned the items were still in the garage. I negotiated a price for the whole lot for 50 cents per book and a nickel per card and headed off to rent a U-Haul trailer.

Now, in hindsight, I wish I had been selling on Amazon at the time, but alas I was only selling on eBay. My cost was $1,340. My net over the next several weeks totaled over $7,000! I had just learned that new items can be a treasure also. The greeting cards I sold in lots of ten starting at $2.99, and often the bidding went over retail price. Who would have thought?

10 ZEPHYRHILLS AND THE SNOWBIRD LEGACY

Capital One brought us to Florida, but the entrepreneurial spirit was not dead in me. I was just not cut out for corporate America, so within months both my wife and I had resigned our positions and were working hard at making a living on eBay. During the next few months I discovered auction houses and costume jewelry. Upon resigning Capital One we moved from Tampa to Zephyrhills, Florida. This quaint community is best known for its bottled spring water. I never saw the springs or the bottling plant. I did, however, see hoards of old people. The population of Zephyrhills quadruples during the winter months when all of the snowbirds from up north move down to avoid the cold weather. These are my peeps.

This 'snowbird' phenomenon causes businesses to open for the winter and close for the summer. It also creates a huge inventory of antiques and jewelry at the local auctions, as many snowbirds don't make it through the winter, sadly enough. As we started attending the auctions, we discovered that competition was fierce for the jewelry lots in the beginning, but as the auctions progressed, deals were available. By hanging around to the end of the auction, my wife and I were able to purchase large amounts of jewelry for chump change. We would buy jewelry boxes full of costume jewelry, sort through it, pull out all the name brands, and return the remainder for auction sale in subsequent weeks. We found we could often sell the remains for more than our original buy price by having the items available for sale in the first auction of the month.

Many of the buyers were seniors on a fixed income and more inclined to bid higher earlier in the month. This fact has proven true throughout numerous auction venues over the last 17 years.

It was through these jewelry purchases we achieved our first $5,000 eBay sales month in 1999. However, our average sale was only $5, so fees were taking a significant portion of the profit margin. I was determined to raise my average sale price to $10 within a year. Doing so was harder than we thought. The only way was to increase the value of the listing, as selling in higher quantities (as in lots) had created a negative effect.

We simply had to buy the earlier lots that were for sale, as they had higher value items in them. However, as mentioned earlier, the competition for these higher lots was fierce. We were quickly outbid, and there just did not seem to be any margin left for profit. We were once again discouraged. It appeared we had hit another brick wall.

A few weeks later, I decided not to bid. I had my wife bid while I checked out the competition. I soon found out there were two bidders who were colluding to drive up prices when my wife bid. But if just the two of them were bidding, one would cease and let the other have it for a steal. I devised a plan to thwart them. Armed with all of our savings we proceeded to outbid everyone on jewelry, sometimes paying more than it was worth. In a few short weeks our two competitors gave up. The last time I saw them they were yelling expletives about my wife and swearing off that auction. A few weeks later I saw them pull up and, when seeing my wife, pull right back out. Basically, it had gotten too hot in the kitchen for them. If the truth be known, if they had held out a couple of weeks, our savings would have been exhausted and we would have been the ones to crumble.

11 MY BIGGEST SCORE ON EBAY

Thank You, Winston Churchill.

During our auction-oriented business in Zephyrhills, I did have one moment that has eclipsed all others to date. It was a typical auction, so we went over to preview the items two hours before it started. On the main table was a collection of porcelain Toby mugs from England. A very nice collection, it represented different manufacturers both vintage and current. Since I once collected Tobys, I was very interested. My wife observed me looking at several and asked about my interest, so I explained it to her. We proceeded to check out the jewelry and left shortly thereafter. As luck would have it, our babysitter cancelled, and I decided to stay home with the boys. My wife attended the auction by herself.

When she came home, she was all excited about her jewelry purchases and, as an afterthought, brought out a Toby she bid on and won for me in appreciation of me staying home with the boys (price $55). I was touched, but as I am always willing to sell any material thing, I quickly looked it up on eBay. There were none to be found. Ever the constant gambler, I listed it that weekend starting at $85, and we headed to Jacksonville to visit family. On the trip I kept having a strange feeling and couldn't wait till I got to her sister's house so I could check our auctions. When I checked my auctions, I was dumbfounded. Four hours into the auction, it was already at $885 with only two bidders! A Google search produced nothing. Three days later it sold for $1,920! I was ecstatic.

As I was sending the invoice through PayPal, my phone rang. It was the backup bidder, and he was offering $35,000 for the mug. He was a surgeon from Chicago and was in surgery at the time the auction closed. Believe me, I was tempted to sell it to him, but my conscience wouldn't allow it. I agreed to contact the winner and see if he would part with it.

For two days the winner didn't respond. Then the PayPal payment came through, and he called me. He was in a small town in Maine and had played high school football against me -- small world. Anyway, he was unwilling to part with the item and stated he would mortgage his house first. He was one of the foremost collectors of Toby mugs in the world and had even published a book on them. He sent me a copy of the book, and it explained the value of the mug.

It appeared there were only three of this Winston Churchill mug ever made by this company. Evidently, the war with Germany broke out, and the company was unable to gain permission from the Churchill administration to produce further prototypes. It was not even supposed to exist. The collector from Maine had a copy of a Polaroid in his book that showed the only one previously known to exist, and it was cracked. Under the photo was the word 'priceless.' Evidently, it was worth at least $35,000.

Let me explain something. If the surgeon had been on a cruise, it would have sold for $85, and I would have never been wiser. If the collector from Maine hadn't bid, it would have sold for $85, as they were the only bidders. Many say "oh wow, you could have made $35,000!" I prefer to look at it that I sold something for $1,900 that we only paid $55 for. I am a strong supporter of the glass half full versus the glass half empty theory. I prefer to live life with a smile on my face instead of worrying about the 'what if's.'

12 THE NIGHTMARE ON THIRD STREET

After a year in Zephyrhills we moved to Jacksonville, Florida, so my wife could help her sister run the family restaurant. What was supposed to be a mutually beneficial endeavor ended up being indentured slavery. I strongly recommend individuals second guess the opportunity to work with family members. In my opinion it often leads to disaster, and this was one such case.

13 MY CASINO OPINIONS

In 1998/1999 I found myself the primary child caregiver while my wife slaved 60 hours a week. A need to make money at home was apparent, so I started looking for online opportunities. I tried everything available from clicking on ads to search engine searches for pennies on a dollar. At one time, I had seven search bars taking up 3/4 of my computer screen and two online radio stations that paid me to listen. My hourly rate was about $5 an hour jumping through these hoops. To save my sanity I started signing up for free gambling accounts to play. After a while I found a website called My Casino Opinions. They offered a free $20 coin to use at different casinos if you would keep track of your experience and write about it when complete. It sounded like fun, so I jumped right in.

Over the next six months, I signed up for and wrote opinions on 45 different casinos. I quickly became the highest rated writer and was soon offered up to $200 each from casinos wanting me to write about them. I treated it as a business and kept a binder on my play at every casino. I ended up winning at 43 out of 45 casinos by doing this. Using their money to play, it is hard to lose. At the time play thru requirements were only 8 to 1. In other words, if the casino gave you $50 to play, you had to place a total of $400 in wagers before you could cash out. Slots were killers, and very seldom could you hope to cash out before losing it. Blackjack was a whole different story. If you play it by the book, cutting out emotion and hunches, the house advantage was only 2%. So for every $100 wagered, you would on average lose $2. So in the case above, you would still have $42 after wagering the $400.

Often I would cash out half the winnings and play the rest in slots. At one casino I ended up cashing out $17,000. At another, $12,000. At the one I cashed out $17,000, I had at one time been at $35,000, so in my wife's mind I lost $18,000, while in reality I won $17,000. I mention this because it is extremely important that any entrepreneur who wants to be successful have a supportive spouse or family. To this day my ex-wife expounds I lost money doing this, when in all reality I won about $35,000 over that period.

14 9/11 THE DEATH OF ANTIQUES

In July of 2000 I finally opened our own antique store. I did it in what I thought was a partnership with a local Silestone (Quartz countertops, like granite but better) fabricator and distributor. The concept was he would create a kitchen in the back with Silestone and would fabricate several pieces to cover the tops of antique dressers/phone stands/occasional tables, etc. I would in turn sell the fabrications for a commission of 30% and hopefully get some kitchen design orders also. He never delivered a single piece, and I was stuck with an antique shop that was supposed to pull my wife out of her then indentured servitude at the restaurant.

Instead, 9/11 happened. Sales tanked, and I ended up selling on eBay at the shop to wile away the hours. On average, I had two customers a day and, to be honest, did not really have the motivation to sell anything. I soon realized how much I liked selling online and not having to deal with buyers directly. People simply bid, and if they won, they got it.

I do remember getting a phone call one morning from a young man whose grandmother had evidently purchased a ton of beanies during their heyday, some even from me. Well, he brought them by the shop. They were stored in nice flat roller cases that would slide under the bed, seven filled with Beanie Babies, four filled with Beanie Buddies. The latter I had never sold but had seen before. She just wanted them gone so I checked the going price on eBay, which at the time was $1 each. I offered her 50 cents a piece, and the offer was accepted. That week, in front of my desolate antique shop, I set out shelves of beanies, and in a three hour period each and every one of them sold for $3 each or 2 for $5. I only mention this to show that even in a down market, if you buy right you can make money. Also, my shop itself had its best weekend ever because of all the customers who stopped to look at the beanies and wandered in.

During this period I learned to take losses in stride and that money is made in the buying. If you buy it right, you can almost always sell it. I learned from my real estate career (or lack thereof, lol), the buyer is in control. Many people do not understand this. In the case of houses, you only have one house to sell -- yours! The buyer, on the other hand, has literally hundreds of properties to choose from. This became my mantra, and over the past 13 years I have been in charge of the deals I make. I determine price and terms, not the seller. If the deal is not attractive, I do not make it. I do not have to buy anything. Don't misunderstand me, I have made bad deals. I just try to learn from my mistakes and move on.

15 STORAGE AUCTION FLIPPING

Over the next couple of years, my income was pretty much totally derived from eBay and storage auctions, the latter nothing like the shows on television. I first learned about storage auctions from, believe it or not, a yard sale. It was on a Sunday afternoon. I was completing my rounds when I saw a hand drawn sign. As I pulled up, I saw a yard full of boxes. Rummaging through the items I saw a lot of junk mixed with good stuff. When I questioned the seller, she said they did not have time to go through the boxes that they bought at a storage auction and were selling all the excess they didn't want or couldn't use.

She happily told me they had already doubled their money and already had plenty of items for their house. She offered to sell me the whole lot, but I settled for cherry picking and buying items for pennies on the dollar. She had no idea what she had and didn't care -- they had made money, and I loved that attitude. From that point forward I went to storage auctions weekly. ;)

My approach to storage auctions was simply to bid on what I see and let the hidden treasures provide the gravy. It never failed me. I would mentally add up in my head what I could net on what I could see, and I limited my bidding to that amount. As a result of this buying method, I never failed to make money on a storage auction bid. On numerous occasions I sold more items out of the unit to pay for my cost, then I bid even before proceeding to the next unit being offered. That was the business model of some attendees, and I for one was more than happy to work with them.

You want that ugly couch, give me $20, TV set $50, etc. I also flipped complete units after pulling the items I wanted, allowing the treasure hunters to tear into the boxes looking for the elusive gold. I am sure on one occasion I missed out on some home runs. The important thing is I always made money. Secret of a successful business model -- make money!

A word of advice on purchasing at storage auctions: be prepared to work. It is not the treasure that is the problem. It is the junk. You will most likely need a truck or a trailer to haul away the excess. If you want to try this venue, I recommend you hook up with a local auction, flea market vendor, or charity. If you can find someone to come and clean out your unit after you have removed the treasure, that is invaluable. Once I purchased five separate units for a grand total of only $330, and although I made over $1,000 off the unit, it took me five days to clean it out and several trips to auction houses, flea markets, and the Salvation Army. When it was over I came to the realization it was too much work, and my storage auction days were over. :(

Storage auction tip: bring plenty of money. During one storage auction there were eight units for sale. As we approached the final unit, I was feeling pretty good, as I had already purchased three of the seven units and had spent $745 of the $1,000 I brought with me. This last unit was huge, 20' x 20' with doors on each side. Visible to the naked eye were two go-carts, two quads, two dirt bikes, several high end bikes, two jet skis on a trailer, and at least 100 boxes. This unit only went for $700 as there were only three of us left at the auction. I wasn't even in the bidding as it started at $500. The other guy ran out quick, and the third guy won it cheap. I saw him the next day while cleaning out my units. He told me he was sweating it on the bidding because he only had $800. Point of the story: I could have won that unit worth $5k or more if I had only brought more cash. :(

Note: For those of you that don't know me, I am typing this sentence on the 11th deck of the Carnival Dream looking over the lush landscape of Roatan, Honduras. I love arbitrage, and the freedom it gives me. ;)

16 ANOTHER ONE BITES THE DUST

Marriage, that is....

The date is 4 Oct 2003, and I am receiving my MBA, Master's Degree in Business Administration. I am eager to start my new career in hospital administration, civilian style. Instead, I learn my wife walked out of the ceremony half way, taking my two sons with her. Upon arriving home I am told she wants a divorce, and I am to get out! Another one of the many pitfalls of being an entrepreneur.

Not all individuals can handle the roller coaster ride that accompanies having your own business. I cannot stress enough the importance of this being a mutual decision. In my humble opinion, the most important asset to a successful business model is a supportive spouse. The opposite is also true.

So, America, what do I do now? I do what any red-blooded man who loves his family does. I apply for a job with the Secret Service and return to D.C., the traffic, the cold, the stress. Three short months later I get a FedEx envelope with the divorce papers. My last ditch attempt at saving my marriage by "getting a job" was unsuccessful. So, here I am in D.C., a place I loathe, doing a job I don't want, and my wife (oops, ex-wife) and sons are living the life on the beach in Florida. NOT!

I give my two weeks notice, pack up my truck, and return to the land of sunshine, bikini clad women, sand, and surf... Well, actually, no surf. I cannot swim and prefer not to expire from this earth in the jaws of a shark, so my appreciation of the ocean is mainly visual. Finding a place to live is a challenge, though, as I gave the wife and her mom both houses at the beach, all furniture, belongings, etc., from the marriage.

What did I get? I took four suitcases and a smile and faced the world head on.

So, it is now 2005. I have recently bought a couple of condos with financing based on my eBay earnings. Life is good. I am buying and selling up a storm both on eBay and at an auction in Nahunta Ga called Wild Bills. The patronage is very similar to the flea markets in the mountains of Virginia. Everyone is family, cousins married to cousins. My best friend at the time is a man named Tommy. He has been married five times and now lives with his mother here at the beach.

Tommy and I team up and everything I find that is marketable but not on eBay, we take to Wild Bills auction house. It is fairly lucrative, and as my teenage son says, I am making bank. For the next two years life is good. I own two condos, make monthly trips to Biloxi, Mississippi, to gamble and spend as much time as possible making sure my children know they have two parents.

My love life is off and on. There are not that many women today that are attracted to a man who looks like a cross between an Ewok and a Koala bear. Cute, but few swoon in my presence. Cosmo magazine did a survey, and the number one trait that women are looking for in a man is a sense of humor. They want to laugh. If that is true, there should be a line around the block waiting to date me. The mere site of me brings fits of laughter from prospective dates. I am comfortable with my looks, why aren't they? Evidence of this phenomenon can be found on dating sites. As women set up search criteria just as men do, if I put I am 5'8", I am seen by ten times as many women as if I put 5'7". Adding to my dismay are all the women who are less than 5'2", wanting only to view men between 6" and 7" tall. Does all that extra blood pumping through those tall bodies flush out all the other impurities in the human body? Are tall people more intelligent, nicer, better providers, richer? I know not, but evidently women do. :)

17 HURRICANE KATRINA – THE REAL ESTATE BUST

In August of 2005 Hurricane Katrina hit the Gulf of Mexico. The loss and devastation was felt all along the gulf shores. It also had a devastating effect on the whole state of Florida. Not so much the damage caused by the storm, but the subsequent loss of tourism, decline in residential sales, and increase in insurance costs. This storm compounded the decline in housing starts and viability of investing in real estate. Over the next year, HOA fees increased, and occupancy rates decreased. The general malaise of the economy was especially strong in the Sunshine State.

As a real estate investor, I prided myself on my knowledge of real estate conditions. Although I was not a doom and gloom prophesier, my handle is recession-fighter. I was convinced for several years that a correction was coming both in the general economy and real estate in general. My belief was that when the hammer fell, prices would plummet. I was like a soap box politician. My mission in life was to warn the world. Every yard sale was an opportunity to educate the masses.

Every time I went to a moving sale, I was amazed by homeowners who were selling their homes to buy larger ones way out of their price range. Couples were buying homes for $400k plus on combined incomes of as little as $70k. Were they insane? I would explain, if interest rates rose, there would be no market for selling their new home. How many people in the Jacksonville area could afford a $4000 a month mortgage, which is what would happen if interest rates rose to even 9+1/2%?

18 ANOTHER ATTEMPT AT 9-5

Or in this case, 11-8.

As stated, Hurricane Katrina was having a devastating effect on the economy in Florida. I felt the urge once again to pull up my britches and re-enter corporate America. I applied for a job with State Farm to become an insurance adjuster and underwriter. To my amazement I was accepted. Eleven months of paid training at $12 an hour during training. I was rich..... NOT! My first check, to my chagrin, was all of $747. For two weeks! How could a man with an MBA forget such things as taxes and Social Security? I had been out of the workplace so long, this man forgot.

Needless to say, things were rough. The mortgage on my condo alone was $1,200 a month. Couple that with HOA and utilities, etc., and I was paying $1,800 just on my condo. It was apparent the income from the training was not going to be enough to make ends meet, so I started looking for supplemental income online. Of course, most opportunities were scams. This happened so much I automatically typed in the business name and "scam" in search boxes before I would even read the proposal.

Well, my latest love interest called and asked if there were any Popeye's chicken restaurants on her way home. I accessed the internet and, after telling her the location, noticed a banner ad had popped up offering a $500 gift card for Popeyes. "Who would want a $500 gift card to Popeyes?" I thought. Intrigued I clicked on the ad and learned what you received was a $500 prepaid ATM card, and all you had to do was sign up for a few offers online. Hmm, interesting.

Now, for the fine print. In order to get the ATM card, you needed to sign up for one silver offer, two gold, and three platinum, in that order. The first page of silver offers were displayed. The first offer was for a trial membership in Match.com. Hmm, things were not working out with my present relationship. It couldn't hurt so I quickly signed up. Wow, only $10. If I could find five more dating sites for $10 each, I would soon have $500 to spend on those dates. Hey, maybe love was in the air.....

As my usual luck would have it, when I went to the next page and the gold offer were displayed, there were no dating sites, just several travel organizations and the minimum cost was $69.99. I quickly saw where this was going and turned off my browser. When I received my second huge paycheck from State Farm I got re-motivated and started searching again.

I typed "free money" in the search bar, and the first thing that came up was a program titled Project Payday. It stated that if I would sign up for one of the online offers under them, they would send me an e-book on how to make thousands of dollars a month online. I took the bait, and low and behold, the first offer I saw was only going to cost me $1, another dating site called True.com with a 30 day trial. It had to be fate.

I downloaded the book and read through it voraciously. The premise was that there were literally hundreds of websites out there that were making money, providing advertising. As an example you could sign up for the website Cokerewards.com and sign up for an offer and basically double your money. If the trial period cost $20 they would pay you $40.

Let me explain. Let's say the offer was for a Blockbuster membership at $19.99 per month. If you signed up under their link and paid for the membership, they would put $40 in your PayPal account. Why would they do this? Because Blockbuster was paying them $75 for each new referral. If you cancelled during the trial period you would be up $20.01. If you signed up for all of the offers currently displayed on Cokerewards.com, you stood to earn a couple of thousand dollars in less than a month. All you had to do was remember to keep a log and make sure you cancelled the item before the yearly membership kicked in. Now, that was where the fun began. Cancelling some of these memberships was worse than a trip to the dentist. Remember when you first cancelled AOL? Ouch.

Anyway, the real money was in referring others. Once you signed up for one offer on each of these referral sites, you were than allowed to refer others. How it worked was if you got someone to sign up for Blockbuster under your referral ID, you would be paid $60, out of which you paid the referral $40, pocketing $20. Project Payday had an extensive list of referral websites and several forums that people used to sign up new referees. It was outlined in great detail, so I tried it out.

Doing this program was e-mail intensive, and at the time there was no wi-fi. I found myself racing to Taco Bell each 30 minute lunch break to wolf down a couple of tacos while my laptop logged on to the internet they provided. I would open my e-mail, respond to a bunch of questions, and haul butt back to class. For brevity's sake, let's say it was rough. I was late a few times, and the instructors were not very happy.

Two weeks into signing up for Coke Rewards and several other referral programs, my earnings were already over $2,000. My first disbursement from Coke Rewards was for $1,340 and arrived the same day I got my third paycheck from State Farm for $747. You do the math. My attempt at re-entering corporate America once again failed, and I gave my two weeks notice. Online entrepreneur was calling and I, for one, was going to answer.

19 KATRINA AFTERMATH AND A TOTAL LACK OF CONFIDENCE

During this time I was investing in real estate. Armed with what I believed was a correct assessment of the market, I used my earnings to invest in lower priced properties, condos to be exact. My thought was: "Real estate crashes, people still need a place to live, they will downsize." I focused on condos under $100k. Well, real estate did crash, and people lost their homes, in that I was correct. But I did not anticipate the devastating after effects of Hurricane Katrina and how long it would last. Because of skyrocketing insurance costs, HOA fees skyrocketed. Positive cash flow went to negative cash flow.

Condo values went from $120k to $40k, sales were stagnant, and evictions were on the rise. Every renter was behind on their rent, and being the consummate nice guy I let them until I could no longer make my mortgage payments. My house of cards crashed down around me. With my savings wiped out, I approached the banks with properties that still had a little equity in them. The banks literally slammed the door in my face. They were unwilling to believe the market would go lower. Result: bankruptcy.

20 HOMELESS AND ALONE

So, in 2007 after the banks foreclosed on my condos, I was homeless and alone. I still sold on eBay, but with no place to live or work and no capital, my sales were minuscule. I traveled from relative to relative doing remodeling in exchange for room and board. I was a college graduate with three degrees and no job prospects. At one point, with no other options, I lived in a garage with a dirt floor, unfinished walls, and no plumbing. I wasn't alone, though. I got to share these luxury accommodations with a couple of snakes, a dozen or so spiders, and a rabid possum who thought I was the invader. I was taking showers at the base gym. I had hit dirt bottom, literally.

My daughter, who was and still is my best friend, had moved to Texas a year earlier. I had helped her move then, and now she needed my help again. Her marriage had failed, and she needed to move herself and her sons into a smaller home. I love Texans, but I hate Texas weather. Temperature changes of 60 degrees or more in a single day are not unusual. But my daughter needed my help, so I packed up my truck and headed west.

The first thing I noticed in Texas was the size of its population. Not in numbers, but in height and girth. The first time I went to a dollar store, there were two beautiful Texas ladies operating the cash registers six feet apart. As my cashier was trying to open her register so was the lady behind her. It was hilarious. They kept bumping into each other like those balls that swing in perpetual motion. Neither could gain any ground. I was the only one laughing, and from the looks I got from other customers my sense of humor was not appreciated. Let's simply put it this way, there are very few all-you-can-eat buffets in the state of Texas. The chances of me meeting a future Ewok/Koala bear mate were very slim in the land of giants.

Trying to do eBay for a living was not working out in the Lone Star State. Yard sales were few and far between -- and when I say 'far between' I mean miles, as in 20 or 30. Also, Texans tend to value and keep their good stuff and only get rid of the oddball items or junk. Used clothing, used dishes, and pots and pans abounded. I often wondered if individuals just got tired of doing the dishes because more often than not they still had food on them....

Because of the scarcity of sales, it was not unusual to need to park 1/4 of a mile away to finally arrive at the sale and see two undocumented citizens fighting over a stained shirt or rusted frying pan. To say that the Texas yard sales I visited were not going to produce eBay home runs was an understatement. So off to the local fleas I went with a dollar in my pocket and a grin on my face.

I need not have wasted my time. If you live in the Dallas/Fort worth area, you do not need to drive several hundred miles to visit Mexico. Just go to the nearest flea market. It quickly became apparent that I had to change my language, my heritage, and my selling platform to eBay Mexico, or seek another line of work. So the remodeling business card came out of the mothballs.

Ever the entrepreneur, I spent the winter remodeling for pennies on the dollar of what I used to charge in D.C. However, it seems every visitor from the south is a custom craftsman well capable of doing almost any remodeling task for $10 to $15 per day. So although I had made many friends, the sandy beaches of Florida were calling this wayward son home, like a siren on the waves.

21 PLENTY OF FISH AND A RED-HEADED GYPSY

Armed with the knowledge I was heading east as soon as the snow melted, I started surfing the web in search of prospects. Applying for jobs on Jaxjobs, I kept seeing a dating website banner called "Plenty of Fish." How appropriate I thought. I am returning to the sea, and this site says there are plenty of fish, unlike the present southwestern desert I presently abide in. With renewed optimism I created my profile and cast out my line. Over the next week I got a few nibbles and even an occasional bite. I guess with a profile like mine, there was not going to be a feeding frenzy. The market for jobless, homeless, penniless losers seemed to be pretty slim. You see, unlike the rest of the patrons on this site I was brutally honest. I was determined to present the facts, unlike the competition who expounded on their Harley, their sailboat, their McMansion or six figure incomes and bank accounts.

After a couple of weeks of extremely limited responses, I decided to go from a cane pole to a fishing net and include fish older than me. Whoa, hold on, I hadn't been looking for fish ten to twenty years younger, just one to five. So in a stroke of divine influence, I changed my profile to include female fish a little more seasoned then myself. Within five minutes I had a strike. Her profile simply said, "Tell me your dreams, and I will tell you mine." How appropriate, as I am such a dreamer. I responded, and an instant friendship ensued. She called me a few hours later, and I headed out the door with my phone in hand. Three hours later my phone died, and I found myself standing in the middle of a cow pasture, ankle deep in cow pie with a dozen cows eyeing me warily. I was smitten.

Exactly one month later, after numerous texts and phone calls, it was decided Cynthia would fly to Texas and ride back to Florida with me. If this budding online romance was to flourish, we had to meet, and we decided to just jump into the fire. Seventeen hours of driving to the east coast would be a testimony to our new relationship.

I booked the flight and eagerly awaited her arrival. We planned to meet at the baggage claim. I waited in the shadows, roses in hand, and when she turned to look at the turnstile I slipped my hand around her waist, placed the roses in her arms, and we shared our first kiss. The sound of our heartbeats was deafening. The rest of the world ceased to exist. It was a storybook moment. To me it was Nirvana. To Cynthia it was, "Oh my god, he is so short," lol. Then she saw my smile, and her defenses fell.

We gathered her bags and headed to the parking garage. As I opened the door for her, I slid my hand to the small of her back, and she melted in my arms. As she slid into her seat, I literally fell to my knees on the hard concrete floor. We hugged, with tears in our eyes. Two soul mates had finally met after 50+ years of searching. The gypsy and the Koala bear. An unlikely match made in Heaven. I thank God for bringing us together. Ok, enough mush, this isn't *Fifty Shades of Grey*. That will be a later book, *100 Shades of Red*, lol.

22 PONTE VEDRA, SAWGRASS

The mountain boy on a golf course.

Did I mention I am not a golf fan? I call it cow pasture pool, and here I am living on the ninth hole of one of the most prestigious golf courses in the world. I have more in common with the gate guards than the golfers who live here. I drive a beat up Ford F-150 with 200,000 miles on the odometer. I change the oil weekly by adding a quart every day that it burns off. Parked between two pristine Jaguars, it is an odd sight. My neighbors are friendly enough, just not my cup of tea. Give me my dysfunctional flea market profiteers.

Over the next few years my arbitrage experience continued in the online world mainly with eBay, Craigslist, and a few books on Amazon now and then. My major source for products is yard sales, which are virtually endless here in Jacksonville. In the summer, there are often community yard sales that have hundreds of houses each participating. If you can cover even half of the sales in a ten mile radius, you are really hustling. I have stopped going to the fleas because the vendors want too much for their wares and constantly have printed eBay listings at their table to justify their prices. Problem is, they have current Buy it Now listings, which are far from indicative of what they sell for online.

During this time period I finally succumbed to technology and bought an internet plan for my little Blackberry cell phone. I believe the cost of internet service was $15 more per month -- I am being dragged into the 21st century dragging my heels, I assure you. That first weekend I went to my first yard sale and looked over the wares. I spotted a bound collection of *The Far Side*, by Gary Larson. The seller wanted $15 for this item. This was far above my comfort zone. As I went back to my truck a little dejected, I accessed the internet for the first time, and on that small screen brought up eBay.

My search of closed auctions showed the lowest price this item sold for was $49.95. Hallelujah, I quickly returned to the seller with the book in hand. Armed with this new found information, I negotiated the price down to $12. My first purchase using this new technology already paid for two months of internet service. A new world had been opened to me, and I now had the tools to bring my sourcing to a whole new level.

Armed with instant access to eBay at my fingertips, I soon found more items to buy than I had funds to purchase. That night over dinner, Cynthia offered me $500 from out of her sock drawer, and from that point on she became my banker. Approaching next week's sales with a fat wallet, I was a force to be reckoned with. Gone were the jitters when buying something for $100 or more. This was business. Within thirty days, I turned the $500 into $3500 and paid Cynthia back plus another $500 in interest. I now had a strong supporter behind my eBay endeavors. :)

Over the next few years, time, space, and capital restraints limited my sales on eBay to $5k to $8k per month, which equated to $3k to $5k per month net. Not a bad income for a one man operation operating out of a small condo with the duchess. Oh, did I forget to tell you? Cynthia is more of a duchess than a gypsy, and the constant influx of product into our home was a constant source of discord, and on more than one occasion knocked our romantic train off the tracks. There just has to be another way, a better way, I thought.

Book Two:

The Adventure Continues, I See a River

23 FLEA MARKETS REVISITED

It is now July of 2010. I have rented a second condo to try to have room to do eBay. My sales are running approximately $7,000 per month. I have hit another ceiling. Although I have space, I cannot find enough product to sell. I am now attending three auctions a week, going yard saling on Fridays and Saturdays, and hitting flea markets on Wednesdays and Sundays. My typical ROI is about 100% so I am netting roughly $3,000 a month and easily working 60 to 70 hours per week. I just cannot see how to bust through this ceiling. Others are doing worse than me.

Every Saturday morning I go yard saling. As I explain to friends and family, 90% of my money is earned on Saturday. I typically spend between $1,500 and $2,000 on a Saturday sourcing at yard sales. My friend, Brian, another eBay-er is my heaviest competition. We meet most Saturdays at 2:00 for Chinese buffet and to tease each other about our booty. He invariably spends a little over a hundred to my couple of thousand. He is amazed I can find so much product despite the fact we go to the same yard sales. Often I am right behind him. I listen as he brags how he bought this item for $5 and expects to get $30 and several other items the same way.

His typical ROI is about 200 to 300% so he is earning about $300 to $350 per week. When I show him my loot he invariably says, "Oh, I saw that. I could have bought it, but it is not worth it."

Brian is stuck on the concept that he must at least double his money so he makes $300 a week and I make $800 to a $1000. He is quick to point out that I have to work a lot more hours then him, and he is correct. Problem is, $300 is not a living wage for most families in this day and age, and so he was forever having financial difficulties. He was eating McDonald's while I dined on cruise ships. Which one would you rather be?

24 THE ART OF NEGOTIATION

I would be remiss if I did not include a chapter on the art of negotiation. These techniques have worked for me for 20 years. If possible, always try to get the seller to quote a price first. Often times the price was less than I was willing to pay. If there is a price, ask if they would consider something less. You can use the excuse that you are buying it for a child, grandchild, parent, etc. Try to make a connection with the seller. I remember when I was first yard saling in Florida, my young son would go with me. Invariably as we would approach the sale, the women at the sale would tell him how cute he was and often offer the item he chose at the sale to him for a reduced price or free.

I soon learned that having him bring the item up to the seller often resulted in a reduced price without even asking. Some might say I was exploiting him but I prefer to state I was teaching him a lesson about life. :) Returning to negotiating, if the sale is a moving sale, I will ask them where they are moving to. I try to establish rapport. It is then I explain what I do and that I have to work within margins. Often times they will offer me the whole lot or a substantial discount for purchasing a large amount.

In individual negotiating, I will usually offer a price between 25 and 50% of what I am willing to pay. Let's say a seller is asking $25 for an item that I need to acquire for $15 to meet my margins. I will first ask if he would consider taking less. Based on his return comment I would explain my business and ask if he would consider $10, allowing him to counter with $18 or $20, my goal being the $15 price point I need. If I cannot get the seller to lower the price point I need it to be at, I will look around for a small item to make up the difference and ask them to please throw that in and I can meet my margins. If you are friendly this will often do the trick. If they will not part with that item, perhaps there is something they will part with that will enable you to get where you need to be.

In the art of negotiating, I cannot stress enough the importance of treating the other person with respect. It is my goal when I walk away for the seller to feel they got a fair deal and want to deal with me again. My friend, Brian, on the other hand wants the seller to think he is the cheapest man on earth. He will show up with a pocket full of quarters and basically shame them into giving him the item for almost nothing. It works for him a lot of times, but I cannot see those people looking forward to repeat business with him.

Another method I will use is kind of like what the short guy on the "American Pickers" television show does. I will bundle things. When you have a particularly tough seller to negotiate with, this will often work. Put several items together, and ask if he will negotiate on the whole lot. Let's say you have $150 in items priced separately, you can normally negotiate the amount down to $125 or lower.

25 LEGOMANIA

I would estimate I have sold probably $50,000 in Legos over the years. It is a phenomenon that has not died like Beanie Babies. In fact many Lego mini-figs are worth more than their weight in silver and may be approaching the value of gold. The majority of my purchases for Legos were at yard sales, but I have purchased a few large lots on Craigslist. As a matter of fact, there is a gym bag full in my office that I purchased for $50 just this past week. One of my old contacts called me and asked if I still bought Legos. I said sure and we met. I opened the bag, did a cursory search, and offered him $50. He was happy, and so was I.

When I was called the Lego man, at the fleas I was known for offering $3 a pound and $1 a piece for mini-figs. This was for clean Legos without a lot of junk and no Bionicle, K-nex, or Mega Blocks in the lot. If it was a mixed lot I would offer $2 a pound or I might go $3 if I saw some mini-figs I liked. Mini-figs are the Holy Grail of Legos. One time I bought a Batman set that had Mr. Freeze in it at a yard sale. The set had a $5 Goodwill sticker on it but the homeowner was selling it for $10 and would not budge. If I remember right, it was missing two mini-figs. I purchased it and another bucket I got her to throw in for $5. As luck would have it the missing mini-figs were in the bucket. The set sold for $125 on eBay even though I put 95% complete because even then I did not have time to build sets. I simply took several pictures of the Legos and the mini-figs and said may be missing pieces.

Over the next few years I bought thousands of dollars worth of Legos from a man at the flea market. He was buying them at a local Goodwill for 10 cents a pound. One time he called me all excited.

He had eighty pounds and 235 mini-figs. People were amazed when I handed him five crisp Benjamins ($500) and told him to keep the change. My friend Brian shook his head in dismay. I ended up selling those Legos for over $2,000. Today Brian is an avid Lego hunter. :)

Another Lego story cost me a job, boo hoo, not. I was on my way to an interview to go to work for Prudential insurance. I was all dressed up nice and purty, wearing a suit and tie. As I was driving down the road I saw a yard sale sign flapping in the breeze. It was a Friday, and although I was sure it was probably a week-old sign I figured, what the heck, and pulled a U-turn with my truck. As I approached the sale, I saw a couple in their 50s sitting in lawn chairs in the driveway with two huge Rubbermaid bins and nothing else. I thought to myself "what a waste of time."

Having already made the detour I walked up to the couple and asked how their day was going. They said I was the first person to stop. Several had driven by but nobody actually stopped. When I asked what they were selling they simply stated they were selling the contents of these two bins. Apparently, their son had gone off to college two years ago and was now living in California and had left these behind. They had asked him numerous times to come and get them out of their garage but he never came so they were selling them.

I almost fainted when they lifted off the lid of the first one. It was full of Legos, mainly Star Wars and Harry Potter. The other bin was full of pristine Star Wars paperbacks, full series. Trying to hid my excitement, the mother sheepishly said, "Is $50 too much?" I said, "For each?" She replied, "No, for both." To make a long story short and report that this fairy tale is a true story, I happily gave the couple $100, loaded them in my truck with the father's help, and returned home. I called Prudential and told them I didn't want the job.

Once again, I believe fate diverted me from a job I would have hated. It took me a couple of months to sell off all the Legos and the books. If I recall correctly, I made over $3,000 on that lot. I stopped by that couple's home a few times while out yard saling on future hunts to thank them again, but they were never home.

During this time I met Adrianne at her yard sale. When she saw me looking up her items on eBay, she asked me to please teach her and her family how to do it. I agreed and returned to her house during the week. At the time I charged $50 for a one hour session on how to sell on eBay and would give the client my phone number to call in the future if they had any questions. Adrianne and I talked several times over the next several months and even went yard saling together. She was amazed how much stuff I would buy versus her, and I would explain it was dozens of years of experience. I literally saw profits where she and others could not yet see them. We developed a friendship that is still strong today.

From July to December I worked my tail off, and in December I had one of my better months with sales of nearly $8,000. It is during this month that I had my first epiphany. I had been saving as much as I could during those months and can proudly say I had saved about $10,000. I was considering investing in real estate again, but remembered my mantra: Real estate giveth, and real estate taketh away. I was determined to make something with this money. At this time I met with Adrianne, and she encouraged me to invest in myself. "Take the money and buy more product," she said. Problem was, there was only so much product out there that I could find that I could double my money on. I had hit another ceiling.

During that night I searched and searched for ideas that might make me money. I remembered the glory days of Beanie Babies and the fast cash I made. I remembered that he who has the most money pass through their hands has the power, like the banks. How could I find more product? Then all of a sudden, the answer came to me: Stop being so stingy. Share the wealth. If I could lower my margins, I could easily find more items to buy. My mind was racing with memories of items I had seen at sales and fleas that would provide a nice profit, even if not 100%. Opportunities lost, I thought, and with grim determination I decided in 2012 I would not be so greedy. I would open my arms to the abundance of the earth and share the wealth.

This became my new mantra: Share the wealth. Allow others to make a profit. Stop haggling down so hard. In January I sold $15,000. In February $22,000. By mid-March, my sales were over $30k. It was working. Now, new challenges were arising. Space, time, and energy were but a few. I had hit another ceiling. In disgust I decided to go on vacation. I booked a cruise and eagerly awaited our departure.

26 WHO IS CHRIS GREEN?

The day before the cruise, Adrianne called and asked Cynthia and I to meet her for lunch. She was all excited and asked Cynthia to be sure to bring her iPad. Evidently, she felt she had the solution to my most current growth issues. After ordering coffee and our favorite cinnamon rolls, I patiently let Adrianne explain her plan. Even after selling on eBay for only a few months, she was already bogged down with all of the steps to list, sell, and ship a product using eBay's platform. She had spent the past week exploring new ways to sell online and had come across a book she wanted me to read. She downloaded the book to Cynthia's iPad and made me promise to read it.

Three days into the cruise, Cynthia forced me to read *Retail Arbitrage* by Chris Green. Ten pages into the book, I wanted to jump off the ship. The second Epiphany struck. I was on the wrong platform. FBA was the gamer changer of my life. Fulfillment by Amazon allowed me to leverage my sourcing by assuming many of the mundane tasks attributed to selling online. Adrianne reversed our roles and became my mentor, helping me to get set up with all of the equipment, helping me through the technical obstacles, and being a cheerleader. I cannot repay her or Chris Green enough.

27 TRANSITION FROM EBAY POWERSELLER TO AMAZON PROFITEER

The biggest changes I went through switching from being an eBay seller to Amazon was from sourcing primarily used items to primarily new items. Although I had a vast reservoir of prior items I had sold on eBay, I was just like many a newbie to Amazon. I had to go through the growing pains like everyone else. The main advantage I had was I was able to rule out many potential purchases because of past experiences. I also was able to use my prior contacts to purchase items for Amazon. The main difference now was I mainly wanted new items with a UPC code. As of this typing, I still have not created a listing on Amazon. I have simply piggybacked on the listings already existing.

In March of 2012, I sold $38k on eBay, and in April I sold $41k. The exciting thing was, I also sold $20k on Amazon. I can tell you unequivocally, the $20k was so much easier. Scanning a product, slapping on a label, and packing it in a box is so much easier than taking pictures, uploading them to Auctiva, writing a listing, determining a price, deciding whether to offer free shipping or charge, determining shipping rates when applicable, confirming it sold, relisting if it didn't, sending invoices, hounding buyers, packing each item individually, driving to the post office, wondering whether I should insure or not, answering countless questions (many of them childish in their very nature), sending feedback, responding to feedback, dealing with disgruntled buyers, dealing with PayPal, remembering to have money in my PayPal account to cover fees…the list goes on forever.

28 MY FIRST 18 MONTHS ON FBA

In my first 18 months selling on the FBA forum, I sold $1,057,118.98. Appendix 2 is a breakdown of what I sold, sourcing information, and my COG and ROI, as many say. This is the meat and potatoes that many in the industry want to know to quantify the value of any information I am providing. Once again I want to reiterate, this book is not a how-to book, just the story of how I did it. There are many ways to source for Amazon, and there will most likely be new ways in the future. I hope to explore some of those ways myself in the coming years, but for now will leave the advice on those methodologies to those who have that expertise. :)

True retail arbitrage -- my first sourcing attempt after reading Chris' book -- was to go to a place called DD's Discounts, with Adrianne's brother. While I was on the cruise, her family were already highly involved in scanning retail outlets and thrift stores. Adrianne downloaded the 100 free scan trial of Scanpower to my phone, and off to the store Andy and I went. Ever the gracious person, Andy pointed me to the toys to scan away, and he headed off to other parts of the store. An hour later, he returned with a shopping cart full of items, and I only had two toys in my cart. He had been doing this two weeks, and I had 18 years of experience. Talk about a reduced learning curve...

Thirty minutes later, after checking out the infants section, I had about $200 worth of items in my cart, my phone was dead, and I had used up all of my scans, but overall I felt pretty good about my first scouting experience. We parted ways and made plans to source one of the local flea markets over the weekend. Over the next few days, I scanned Big Lots, Ross Dress for Less, Bealls

Outlet, Target, and Kmart. I spent about $1,000 and was a little nervous -- would this stuff really sell? About this time I realized I had made my first mistake: I had a room full of stuff and none of the equipment to enter the items into Scanpower. I called Adrianne, and she ordered me the necessary tools I would need to get started.

That weekend I took Andy to the flea market. Within an hour he was overwhelmed and just did not see the money through the trees. He was uncomfortable with the haggling, the heat, and the general demeanor of the flea market vendors. Where I could see diamonds, he could only see junk and wanted to return to the air-conditioned comfort of retail arbitrage. We parted ways, and he pursued retail arbitrage while I expanded my search to yard sales, auctions, fleas, and retail. Sadly, Andy no longer sells on Amazon. This is one lesson I hope everyone gets: do not limit your sourcing opportunities, you never know where you might strike gold.

One of the keys to my success on eBay and Amazon is to always be sourcing. I am a firm believer that you need to have your line in the water to catch a fish. Likewise, it is important to scan everything. If I had my way, I would recommend you scan till your phone dies -- that is how you learn. In my first few weeks on Amazon, I quickly learned the value of being there.

It was a rainy Sunday in April, and the flea market was mostly deserted. Half of the vendors either did not show up or had already left for the day. About 15 minutes into my search, I came across a young couple with a baby. They had two tables covered with Hopkins Trailer accessories. Apparently the young man's grandfather had owned a trailer outlet and had passed away a few years earlier. The large items had been sold off with the rest of the business. However, there was a storage unit filled with these accessories, new in box. His mother had been paying monthly for that storage unit and was tired of the expense. She told her son to take them to the flea market and that he could have whatever he got for them. This was their third week trying to sell them, and they were pretty discouraged. They had only sold a few each week.

The likelihood of a buyer showing up to a table at a flea market needing a trailer hookup for a 2006 Nissan Pathfinder, for example, was few and far between. Unlike on eBay or Amazon, where the world is your customer. I explained this to the young couple, but they had no interest in selling online.

Originally they were asking $10 each per item, but by now were only asking $3 each. He quickly offered to sell me the whole lot for $1 per item. I did not hesitate. I pulled the trigger and told him to add them up. There were 1,486 items so I paid them $1,500, and they delivered them to my condo. The average selling price on Amazon ran from $9.95 to $29.95. I had to get qualified to sell in automotive, and it actually was pretty simple. Within one week of sending in my first shipment, I had my investment back. I still have a dozen or so in stock but estimate I made over $15,000 on this one deal alone. I would never have made it if I had sat at home, all comfy and cozy.

Over the next 18 months I found flea markets to be a wealth of sourcing. I still did retail arbitrage, attended a few auctions, and even went yard saling occasionally. I had found that I could live with a 30% to 50% profit margin, and flea markets seemed to have the most items available within those parameters. Flea market vendors were eager to work with me. Many, whom I had dealt with in the past, were resistant. They were heavily ingrained into used toys and antiques. They were dismayed that the "Lego guy" or "eBay guy," as I was previously known, was simply passing by their wares. I made new contacts and built new relationships. When people would ask me what I do for a living I would simply say "I build relationships," and let those words lead me into the conversation.

Sadly, yard sales were becoming a thing of the past. I simply did not have the time. Yard sales are an excellent source of items you can purchase with great margins, and if your time and funding are limited I strongly recommend you start here. However, as my business developed I quickly learned it was much easier to scan in twenty of an identical item than twenty different items. Yard sales normally do not have multiple copies of new items, although anything is possible.

Now yard sales are my hobby. They are my respite from the grind of hard core searching. Treasure hunting at yard sales can be a lot of fun, and finding a home run is not that difficult. I still revel in the 20/1 return on items I find there, but they are so infrequent my business model cannot be sustained by them. So, hi ho hi ho, it's off to the stores and fleas I go...

29 2012 AND 55,000 MILES

With my newfound discovery of sourcing everywhere, I found myself frequently driving 300 plus miles a day for deals. My normal route to the five fleas in Jacksonville covered 150 miles. What about St. Augustine, Daytona, and Gainesville? On a tip, 100 mile trips were the norm instead of the exception. I was meeting people, developing leads, and building relationships.

Hairdressers, beauty salons, anything carrying women's products were quickly becoming my source for my business model. Why not? Who was the consumer in my household? Certainly, not me. Advertisers target women and children. There is a reason for that. Women buy disproportionately for themselves and their children. This was the hidden market I hadn't accessed before.

By summer, 80% of my business was HBA. I had three Avon reps and two ex-Mary Kay reps looking for me every weekend. One purchase I made initially for $15 for a box of discontinued Mary Kay cosmetics netted me $1,500. I was hooked. Once again there was a barrier to entry with these ladies. Their asking price was much more than I could afford to pay and make a profit, but eventually they saw the light and shared the wealth.

Beware of fakes. I sold MAC cosmetics that I was buying from a source at a flea market for over six months on eBay before the first negative feedback came in. After that, it was an avalanche. I ended up refunding everyone whom I could reach. When I confronted the seller, she swore they were authentic, that her sister was a MAC representative in Canada. To make a long story short, it just isn't worth it, so I ended the business relationship.

Over the summer months I was taking my own advice, selling what sells, not what I like personally. Video games and Legos had been replaced by consumable beauty and hair products. I was cornering the market on Olay and L'Oreal. If not for my obvious lack of taste in clothing (not the least bit metro), I am sure my sexual preference would have been questioned. Women are profitable. Find out what makes them tick and provide value, and you will make money.

Diet! What a nasty word, but this word could easily be converted to "profit." Weight loss products abound, and the latest fad will bring a premium if unavailable locally. Even discontinued or no longer popular products can sell well. A case in point: In 1983 I went on the Atkins diet and lost 30 pounds in 30 days. As recently as six months ago, I tried again but no luck, just like the 20 other times in the last 20 years. But it worked once.... Discontinued and outdated methods and products have loyal followings that can still bring a premium if they cannot find them through regular retail channels.

Another area of profitability I was finding were pleasure aids. I won't go into great detail, but once again this is an area where shoppers appear to enjoy shopping online, wonder why... Discontinued products in this venue also have loyal followings. An example I can relate: I was selling a certain product from KY that was selling extremely well. KY changed the name a little and the packaging. Still the same product, same ingredients, but looked different on the box. I received more messages through Amazon on the sale of these products over the next 30 days than all of the messages combined I have received in the last 18 months. Both complaints, and raves, despite it being the same product. This shows the power of the belief system: if a person believes a product will increase their pleasure, it will, and if not, the opposite is true.

30 PROFITABILITY AS IT RELATES TO COST OF GOODS

ASP (average selling price)

Over the course of my first 18 months, my ASP ran around $25 to $27, with my ROI hovering around 35%. Recently, in speaking with other high volume sellers, I think this may be the norm. These are typical results that are to be found out there in the market place. Of course, I had home runs, but in reaching the million dollar level I had mainly singles. When considering products for purchase, I look for a minimum 30% return and an ASP of at least $15. I will buy and sell lower priced items but try to get a higher ROI. Purchases in quantities of less than ten, I shoot for 50% ROI. These are general guidelines. I will test market items and adjust my buying model on the results.

31 $1 AND SIMILAR LOW PRICE ITEMS

I currently have four items in stock that I have 40 or more of that I paid $1 or less for each. They are reaching the point where I will have to pay storage fees on them. They are selling, when they sell, for approximately $8 each, and my ROI is about 250%. I have sold approximately 50% of what I purchased, and I have a return on my investment already. I am considering requesting they be returned to me and creating multi-packs to stimulate sales. Based on their performance, I have adjusted my business model to only purchase and list items I expect to sell in the $10+ range.

32 FLEXIBILITY IS THE NAME OF THE GAME

In June of 2013, my sales dropped considerably. This was a combination of less inventory and lower ASP. Less inventory because I was sourcing less due to mental health conditions: i.e., I was taking lots of vacations! Over the past year I had worked a 60 to 70 hour work week for almost 12 months and was extremely stressed. Believe me folks, it is not worth your health.

Some of my sources had dried up for a variety of reasons: price dropping, unavailability of product, Amazon entering the market, other FBAers now selling, etc. Some of my sources were now selling online themselves. This was not a surprise to me -- I am the one who told them to do it. I believe in abundance, and when these items became unavailable I started to look at other products.

30% of the items I initially was selling a year before without Amazon as a competitor now found Amazon as my main competitor. Often times, I could compete; other times I had to drop my price or risk products expiring before Amazon sold out its massive quantities. In doing so, my ASP went from $25 to $22. This was a tremendous change and significantly affected my bottom line. To keep my margins, I had to source at 20% less than I was paying, and in many cases I was not able to do so. Therefore, less purchases equal less product, equals less sales... Not rocket science.

33 GROCERY

In August of 2013, I re-evaluated my business model and decided to expand my product line. To do so, I needed an influx of cash, space, and help. I had purchased a couple of cases of Progresso soup starter at a dollar store and had seen them sell quite quickly for a 100% ROI. Based on this sale, I started to look into groceries. It was quickly obvious there were profits to be had. But grocery items are much heavier, bulkier, and much more labor intensive.

To expand into groceries, it was obvious I needed help and additional space. I started looking for warehouse space and started putting feelers out for part-time help. Through the grace of my fiancée, I immediately found a work place and, within days, part-time help.

In the first week of August, I went sourcing in a Tuesday Morning store. The clerk was intrigued with what I was doing. One thing led to another, and we ended up discussing her working for me part-time starting in September. My fiancée had located a nice office space with outside access that was only $495 for 12' x 20' with electric, water, and internet included. What a great deal.

Upon returning from another cruise in August, I was eager to get to work and purchased 5 shelf units from Lowe's, on 1 Sept I moved into my new space and returned our home to my fiancée. This one step greatly improved our relationship. Gone were the arguments over my mess, and we have subsequently married and are enjoying marital bliss. I strongly recommend you get a separate space as soon as it is financially feasible.

At the same time I moved into my office space, I made time to become active on the Scanpower Facebook forum. I enjoyed the camaraderie and was actively posting my successes and setbacks. I was climbing out of the hole, and my sales were climbing back up to the tune of $10k more per month. However, it was already obvious in the first two weeks that I needed a larger space, and I started talking with the landlord about a large office across the hall.

Fate intervened once again and sealed the decision for me. In late August, I arrived at my office one morning to find the ceiling had collapsed all over my product, my computer work station, and supplies. It was a crushing set back. $1,500 worth of product was soaked, and it took me a full week to move into a temporary office and get back up and running. As a result, inventory levels at Amazon dropped, and so did my sales. I negotiated a three month free rent in the new larger space and eagerly awaited it to be ready for me to move in.

During September and October, I actively pursued grocery items. As my volume of sales was reduced due to space constraints, I was able to reconcile my books and look into the profitability of this new model. I quickly discovered how much more labor intensive grocery items were compared to HBA. To achieve an ASP of $20+ most products needed to be sold in multi-packs, so I had a much larger volume of items that needed prep work prior to shipping. Poly-bagging and suffocation labels along with expiration labels were now the norm instead of the exception.

Based on the increased time and cost of prepping groceries, it became obvious that I needed a higher ROI for this business model. I started limiting my purchases to products that were smaller and either had a higher ASP or better margins. No longer was I purchasing large boxes of cereal and other large low cost items.

34 EXTREME COUPONING = PROFIT IN GROCERIES

In September 2013, my first full month adding groceries to my listings, I sold about $12k. I now had a list of 123 different grocery store products to source and was adding new items each week, whatever was on sale in a given week at a given store, etc. Problem was, the item would not be on sale the next week, so items were dropping off my list. This was both good and bad. My base of goods to sell was broadening, but this required constant scanning and sourcing. As soon as I had test marketed an item and found it would sell, the item would no longer be on sale.

As October came around, I noticed that items that were on sale seldom had a coupon offer to accompany it. However, within days of the item coming off sale, a coupon offer would appear. The answer seemed to be grab the coupon when you can and wait for the item to go on sale. Hmmm, didn't I use to do this years ago buying for the family? Also, wasn't there a TV show about this called "Extreme Couponing"?

Maybe instead of finding a product that was on sale and going searching for a coupon, instead I would search for coupons and then search the stores for one that had the item on sale. This way I could increase my margins, and broaden my base of products at the same time. If the price of the item minus the coupon would meet my margin requirements, I should pull the trigger.

What were my margins? Originally, as stated before, I was going off the 30% model I had used with HBA. I had learned now that was a prescription for disaster. Shipping and preparation costs for groceries were easily double the cost for HBA. To be truly profitable, I needed a higher ROI. So after much deliberation, I decided on an ROI of 50% and immediately reduced my list of products from 123 to 78 as a consequence. Those other items were simply too labor intensive to work out with the new model. It was evident if I wanted to expand my list, I was going to have to source coupons along with groceries.

35 GROCERIES AT A FLEA MARKET?

As I conducted my normal sourcing trips at the local fleas, I saw more and more vendors selling grocery items. Most of the items they sold were not attractive to my business model because they were heavy (detergents), hazmat (aerosol or alcohol based), or the price was restrictive. I scanned every item I saw and eventually was buying a couple of items from each vendor. Once again, if you will buy 20 sticks of deodorant or 40 boxes of doggie snacks, you should find yourself in a positive negotiating position. Through this type of quantity purchasing you can often get your cost reduced to meet your margins. Most extreme couponers selling at flea markets are not selling high end goods; they are selling items they have very little money in or acquired for free.

Often the items I purchase from these individuals do not meet my normal expectations. I will spend $100 to buy x number of product to establish a relationship with the vendor. Although I may not make great margins I am creating a working relationship for the future. In acquiring groceries in this manner, I saw that flea market vendors are not selling the normal items I have on my list, so we are not competing. When I asked where they got their coupons, I often received a cold shoulder. They were not eager to give up their source.

I just knew they had to have access to coupons they were not using but that I could use for selling on Amazon. It is a different business model entirely. It took several weeks, but after purchasing weekly from a few of the venders, a few agreed to sell me their extra coupons they were not using. An example would be a coupon for $0.50 off a product selling for $2.50. This would not be a significant enough discount for them to try to buy and resell the product in their venue. However, the item sells for $7 on Amazon and purchasing at $2.50 would only net me $0.50 net profit. Using a $0.50 off coupon made my net $1.00, a 100% increase, and brought my ROI to 50%. It is amazing how when you deal in volume $0.50 a piece can make money, especially in multi-packs.

To further explain I will use the example of Beefaroni. In October, Walmart had Beefaroni for $0.75 a can. I was selling six cans for $25 then, mainly to our troops overseas. The net was around $16, a great deal, but an even greater deal was having $1 off three coupons bringing my cost per can to $0.42 or $2.52 versus $4.50 without coupons. Since then, prices on Amazon have dropped and now they sell for $18 a six pack. Net around $11. Prices in the store have climbed to $1 a can, so $6 for six. Still profitable but using coupons, basically puts that money in my pocket.

Now, back to the vendors. Most, I learned, were getting their coupons from newspaper circulars. Each one was acquiring at least 100 circulars per week. A couple were getting circulars from all over the country. In some cases, a coupon might be for $0.50 off here in Florida but $0.75 off in New York. Guess which coupon I would prefer. At any rate, as of this writing I am spending about $200 a week buying excess coupons from these ladies and saving about $700 in their use, for a net of $500 a week. I hope to expand this search both in flea markets and online sources. My goal is to purchase $20,000 a month in groceries by July and to save an average of 20% by using coupons. This would net me $4,000 a month, which I intend to use for all non-Amazon costs, i.e. cost of the coupons, office rent, supplies, gas, etc. I realize this might be a lofty goal, but I learned long ago that if I didn't set goals, I never achieved them.

36 DOLLAR STORES EVERYWHERE

I have always used dollar stores to buy my bubble envelopes to ship small items for eBay. Recently, I have seen more and more items that would sell on Amazon. While in a Dollar Tree today, I scanned a dozen items and five of them showed margins of 300% or more. I may do a test in the next few months to see if this is feasible and worth the time. I did buy 10 PC video games for a dollar at checkout and am sending them in with this shipment. My cost $1, Amazon price $8.37, decent rank, we will see.

Also, I did see Progresso soups again for $1 and in multi-packs the ROI is easily 100%. I am not sure if sourcing dollar stores continuously is a good idea, but it appears there are frequently deals to be had. Family Dollar had the elusive Deuce Gordon Doll just before Christmas, and I along with several others made some nice coin off purchasing that item and selling it on Amazon.

37 BOLOS, BOGOS, AND A BARREL FULL OF MONKEYS

Q4 (Oct – Dec) was already under way before I started directing my sourcing to this phenomenon. Jay Bayne had just founded the Facebook forum called Scanner Monkeys. The site was created to share BOLOs in a group setting. BOLO means "Be on the Lookout." Several times a day, members post hot items or deals they have seen or have done in the past. Other members rush out and buy them. It spread like wildfire, and the opportunity to cash in on this phenomenon was simply too great to pass up. By the end of October, I was chasing BOLOs with the rest of the monkeys. I drove all over the first coast in my pursuit.

My first BOLO search was for the monkey mascot of the group. This was a small 5" version of the scary monkey from the television show "Family Guy." This quickly became a must have for virtually every member of the group, and members were posting their successes and failures in their search. In my first hunt, I located seven of the elusive creatures at Walgreens throughout the metropolitan Jacksonville area. I offered up the extras to other members, and friendships were quickly created.

The true benefit of the Scanner Monkey group is the encouragement and vast level of experience being offered by its members. Jay instituted a fee equal to 10 cents a day, and I can say it is the second best money I have ever spent -- second only to the purchase of the book *Retail Arbitrage* by Chris Green.

Searching for BOLOS is both fun and profitable. It forces you to think outside the box and to step outside your comfort zone. You will search and find items you never in your life would have thought you would buy or would be profitable. Herein is the true benefit of BOLO hunting. You will find other items as you search for the elusive BOLO. You will learn what sells is often what you would least think to buy. National popular brands are available everywhere to everyone. It is often the obscure item that has true value because it is difficult to acquire everywhere.

In the short three month history of this forum, many alpha monkeys have already appeared. Each had their own expertise and value to add to the group. I would like to thank each and every member of this group. You made Q4 exciting and fun, something I forgot to do over recent years. From the head Monkey Jay Bayne, his assistant Cordelia B, to the comic relief of Brian V, I would recommend everyone who reads this book join this forum. It is well worth the cost of membership. The BOLO log itself is probably worth thousands.

Expert Amazon knowledge is often provided by Karin I.B., and Cheri B. Rachel R.L is a virtual traveling scanning machine. JC is a scanning ninja. Peter M is an online guru and wholesale phenomenon. David P and Ryan W have both provided BOLOS I have personally profited from to the extent of thousands of dollars. Andy S and Duane M, are young stud monkeys quickly climbing the ladder. Pay special attention to what these monkeys post, and you will make money. As Chris Green has said in his Spreecasts, this is a unique group. The value here cannot be overstated. There are approximately 500 members in this group at this time, many contribute daily, other lurk, all are awesome. Thank you, each and every one of you.

Prior to the formation of Scanner Monkeys, the majority of my time was spent in the parent group called Scanpower. This is the quintessential group of online Fulfillment by Amazon on the net. It is directed by the leader of this group and my personal shepherd, Mr. Chris Green. Chris' book *Retail* Arbitrage is the most authoritative guide to selling by FBA. He willingly gives his time to us, his flock. If you are new to selling on Amazon, you cannot go wrong by starting with his new book *Arbitrage* and joining the Facebook forum Scanpower. It will greatly reduce the learning curve and will quickly allow you to join the profiteers making money selling on Amazon.

One quick explanation is for the term BOGO. This means Buy One Get One. Maybe buy one get one free or buy one get one half off, etc. The benefit of a BOGO is it may turn a non-profitable item into a profitable item and turn it into a BOLO. Don't you just love jargon? As of this writing, Walmart is offering matches on BOGOs, so if you see an item at another store is offered as a BOGO, you can enhance your deal by taking that ad to Walmart and saving even more money.

An example happened locally in Publix. They had buy one get one Salmon steaks for $3.95, so cost was $1.98 ea. Walmart regularly sells the item for $3.59 each so with the ad you could get them for $1.80 ea. Now I sell these in multi-packs of twelve for $54.99. My net is around $46. Purchasing them at Walmart makes me an additional $2.16 per twelve pack. Not gonna make me rich, it appears, but can definitely add to the bottom line. If you consider I sold 46,000 listings over the time frame mentioned in this book, this would result in an increase in almost $100,000 in sales.

Today I went to Winn Dixie for the first time in months and saw they have BOGOs also. A quick look and I found several items that would net 75% margins on Amazon in multi-packs. Couple that with coupons and you are looking at 100% easily.

38 FUTURE THOUGHTS

First let me reiterate, this book was not intended to teach someone how to sell on eBay or Amazon. It is simply my experiences over the last 20 years sourcing and selling online on these two platforms. If you enjoyed it and value my fatherly advice, I offer the following thoughts be considered about the future of eBay and Amazon.

Aging Of America

As the population of this country ages, so will the average age of buyers on online platforms. I know, three year olds are using iPads, but I have yet to meet one with a credit card, so let's focus on the old folks. In my opinion, this will become the largest demographic purchasing on Amazon. Think about it. Medical science is extending our life spans. The number of people age 60 and above is growing exponentially. The majority of wealth in this country is held by persons over the age of 55.

As these people age and retire, they find they have more time to spend online and are in fact the fastest growing demographic using the internet. Certain products are designed for this group: adult diapers, sexual enhancement aids, diet aids, medical devices, supplements, etc. As people age, driving to a store to purchase some of these items is daunting and in some cases downright embarrassing. To me, it makes sense that as our population ages, more and more seniors will shop online, and this is a demographic you should target.

Legalized Marijuana

Seventeen states, as of the writing of the book, have already legalized marijuana. As of this moment, factions in Florida are petitioning it for a vote, as I type. I am no expert on the drug, but many experts predict this will be the next breakout industry that may rival the impact of the internet. There is surely money to be made as this develops. No, I am not saying sell dope online! I am saying be prepared to recognize opportunities to source items associated with this product, perhaps in the area of manufacture, distribution, cultivation, usage, etc. I do not know but I am willing to bet, there are already items sold online that are directly related to this plant's usage. As marijuana use expands, opportunities for profit will arise. If this is against your conscience, then consider items devised to reverse the trend. Just like there are hangover products and alcohol scanners you can buy across the counter, surely there will be supplements and homeopathic remedies to suppress its effects and addiction. Just don't stick your head in the sand and hope it will go away. Picture it now... You are the first one to sell the marijuana reversal patch -- it sticks on the forehead so everyone can see how much of a dumb ass someone is... oops giving my opinion again, sorry.

Gay Marriage and Alternative Lifestyles

Let's face it, this is one of the hottest topics in our nation today. As a result more and more products will be developed targeting the GLBT (gay, lesbian, bi-sexual, transsexuals) segment of our population. Heck, they even have a group meeting on Carnival cruises. However, I have yet to see a chapel, services, or any meeting advertised for any religion, as of this typing. Although the prevalence of this group is sure to rise over the next few years, I believe it will be a long time before it is considered mainstream. Hence, online ordering will most likely be a preference for members of this group. Recently on one of the forums, one of the members posed the question, "Is there anything you won't sell?" The answers were vast and colorful, some discussion was created, and there were obvious differences of opinion. If this is an area you would not consider selling in, then consider the other side of the coin.

Christianity and other Religions

Yes, I did go there. Heck, if I can discuss drugs, politics, and sex, I can surely mention God. As the morality of this country continues to decline and the economy continues to struggle, more and more individuals are turning to God. I am one of them. So speaking from experience, I have bought several books, t-shirts, crucifixes, etc, since dedicating my life to Christ. My choice, folks -- freedom of religion is still thankfully the law of the land.

My point is, as marijuana and gay marriage become legal, it is apparent that acceptance of these changes by a significant portion of our populace is not going to happen. At the same time that states are changing laws, churches nationwide are reporting unprecedented numbers dedicating their life to Christ.

Other religions are seeing similar growth. What better way to state your opinion, your belief, and back your side of the debate than with your consumer dollars. It is going to happen. You may choose to stay out of the ruckus, but most certainly an increase in consumer spending will occur on these issues.

The Un-affordable Health Care Act

I already covered, sex, drugs and religion; I would be remiss to not delve into politics. First, I am a retired hospital administrator and have an MBA in health care, so I have a little knowledge on the subject and definitely an opinion. As opinions are like a**holes, we all have one, I will simply say, "It Won't Work." Plan accordingly. What has this got to do with Amazon, you ask? Think holistic products. If going to the doctor for a cold is going to cost you $500 to $1,000, you are going to be looking elsewhere for alternatives.

Holistic and preventive medicine will see a marked increase and so will the sale of related products on Amazon and eBay. I am not sure if a book on how to remove a spleen, using a sharp spoon and a bottle of Tequila, will get many sales, but the latest herbal cleanse ideas, I myself would buy right now. Just watch for changes in medicine and sources.

Going Green

President Obama may have been a little early in his promotion of green energy, and the loss of tax dollars would indicate this is so. However, I don't think anyone can deny that as civilization develops its moral compass of the world we live in, recycling and development of green products is the wave of the future.

As new technologies and products become available, a market will certainly develop also. I expect Amazon in particular to be on the forefront of this activity. With the success of items such as MIO water enhancers, I personally think there may be a growing market for using small bottles of this nature to supplement our food supply and distribution of meds. As it stands, my wife often drinks healthy shakes to lose weight. In the future, I would not be surprised to see most of us replacing a meal in this fashion for economic reasons. If you can take a supplement in a bottle of water that gives you nutrients and curbs your appetite and save $10, for example, this may be the wave of the future and a method for ending world hunger.

Advice from Uncle John

As we approach 2014 and this brave new world that is adapting before our eyes, I would offer this advice. Do not rule out any possibility. The world at the end of this decade will surely be much different than what we are seeing now. Just as I remained flexible and diversified over the last 20 years, I anticipate doing the same over the next ten. Watch the world around you, look for trends, watch what your children and parents are doing. These are the consumers of tomorrow. Most of all I wish you all prosperity in 2014. Thanks to all of you who have unselfishly shared your life experience.

Be The Change You want to see in the World… Gandhi

We are the change that we will see in the world. Just by the very fact that you are reading this book, you are part of a new generation of online sellers who see the possibilities that the internet will bring the world. Embrace the technology.

APPENDIX 1 – 25 QUICK TIPS

Show up, pay attention, tell the truth.

Tip # 1 – Be there. You can't find something if you do not look. Put yourself in the position to source. Everywhere there are opportunities to source from yard sales to high end stores. Engage store managers and other sellers, and buying opportunities will arise.

Tip # 2 – Scan everything. Don't let preconceived notions or belief block your opportunities. Many of the items you will be most successful with will be items you have no previous background in selling. Often times they will be items you would never purchase for yourself.

Tip # 3 – Crosscheck items on eBay. If an item does not appear on Amazon or the price seems disproportionately high, check items on closed auctions on eBay. If the item has sold on eBay for what you can purchase it for, you reduce the chance of losing money. In this case I will test market the item.

Tip # 4 – Don't give up. Everyone starts at the beginning. With experience, comes more opportunities. When you first start scanning or sourcing you will find a very small percentage of items to sell, but each time you go sourcing your percentage will increase as you gain knowledge. Each time you research an item that you find is not profitable, your memory will retain that fact, and you will be able to eliminate that item in future searches, thereby honing your skills.

Tip # 5 – Don't be afraid to fail -- that is how we learn. People do not learn from success but from failure. Treat each failure as a learning opportunity, and you will no longer fear it. You will accept it as a challenge to turn things around.

Tip # 6 – If necessary, test items. If you are not sure of an item, test it. Look at it like testing the temperature of the water. Stick your big toe in -- do not dive in. This is extremely important in building confidence and preventing critical failure. It is better to lament over a lost opportunity (as many more will follow) than to suffer financial destruction above your comfort zone.

Tip # 7 – Be willing to learn from others. Read as many books as you can, and try to learn something from each. Even the smallest piece of information can reap huge profits down the line. Don't dismiss something because you have never done it that way.

Tip # 8 – Once you are comfortable with your business model, look for ways to expand. Do not go deep but wide, and diversify. If possible, source multiple channels and sell on multiple platforms, both online and off.

Tip # 9 – The so-called 3 to 1 rule. This has been around for at least 20 years. People in the arbitrage business have used the double your money minimum as a standard for as long as I have been participating. This is a great starting point and a great buying tip. However, when selling, it should no longer apply. Take into account the opportunity cost of money. If you have money tied up in inventory that you could have back in your account if you would accept a lower margin, lower the price, sell the item and reinvest the money in your business.

Tip # 10 – Be willing to accept a loss and move on. The sooner you dump that mistake and use whatever money you can make on the item, the sooner you can purchase and sell profitable items and make yourself whole. That is one tip I often use. If it bothers me, I quickly reinvest, and the minute the new item recovers my losses I am able to put the mistake behind me. With experience you will know this automatically, and you will no longer sweat the small shi*.

Tip # 11 – Be aware of your environment and trends happening around you. Do not get stuck in your comfort zone. I.e., if you are selling toys, try HBA; if you are selling HBA, try groceries, etc. In downtimes, having multiple categories of products for sale will enable you to weather the storms, and believe me the storms will come.

Tip # 12 – Go where the product is. If you live in a location that has few retail stores and you want to do retail arbitrage, plan trips to these places. If you live in the north and yard sales are non-existent during winter months and you like going to yard sales, go south. If you cannot relocate, make the best of where you live. Explore online arbitrage and wholesaling -- do what it takes to get it done.

Tip # 13 – Do not ignore another's knowledge. No one can know everything. As a matter of fact, we as individuals know very little. Do not let your prejudices about others' stations in life block your ability to learn. When you go to a store listen to the clerk. When you go to a flea market, listen to the vendor. Often times they know a lot more about things than you do.

Tip # 14 – Make and build relationships, whether it is making friends with store managers, expressing an interest in a couple who are having a moving sale, or asking a flea market vendor how the sales are going. Showing an interest in others can do wonders. Also, ask the question and then shut up. People like to talk about themselves. Listen and opportunities will abound.

Tip # 15 – Invest a little now to get a lot later. Help another human being out. You will be amazed how once you buy something, you gain credibility with a seller. People trust people they have had past business with. Even if you have to return several times to gain that trust, do it and opportunities will arise.

Tip # 16 – Ask for the sale. I learned this selling real estate. If you do not ask, you do not know if you can get the sale. An example is you find an item selling at a yard sale for $20, but you need to get it for $10 to make it profitable. Don't assume the seller won't sell you the item for that price. They may, even if they were unwilling to come down on another item. Explain your situation and ask. You never know, this may lead to more items being sold to you at a discount. Also, do not assume that just because a seller is high on one item, he will be high on another. Look at every item and ask about prices on unmarked items.

Tip # 17 – Do not hide what you do. In twenty years I have always been up front. This has garnered me favor on so many occasions I cannot remember them all. When someone asked what I was doing I told them with pride. On literally hundreds of occasions, this led to buying opportunities I would have never had if I had hidden my objective.

Tip # 18 – Be real and be honest. Haggling is good, but talking someone down to $5 on something that is worth $50 is just plain wrong. To win in this industry you need to present a win/win opportunity. Do not look at a deal and say, wow, I could have gotten this even cheaper. If you were happy with the price, be happy with the price. Look at the difference as goodwill you have created with the seller. Provide value -- share the wealth.

Tip # 19 – Share the wealth. As your business grows, you will find opportunities to buy larger quantities of product if you are willing to take a smaller margin. I look at this not as profit loss, but sharing the wealth. If you share your business model and margins with your prospective sellers, they are more likely to appreciate your honesty, and in fact, I have had them offer me items for less when they saw how little I was making. It is a rare and awesome deal when two people are trying to give the other a better deal, versus trying to get over on one another.

Tip # 20 – Don't be afraid to pull the trigger. As you gain experience, opportunities will arise where some deals will seem too good to be true. In that case, do your homework. Check Amazon, eBay, and even Google the item. If it appears to be a great deal, go for it. If you still don't feel confident, ask for advice. Myself, Chris Green, and others in the industry are more than happy to lend our experience.

Tip # 21 – Join social networks. These can be a tremendous resource and can help you avoid mistakes. One word of caution: don't spend all of your time on these forums. Limit your involvement, so you can spend the majority of your time sourcing.

Tip # 22 – Be prepared to grow your business and when opportunity strikes take action. For me it was lowering my margins. For others it may be to move into online arbitrage or wholesale arbitrage. Whatever it takes, do it. Do research, learn from others, and stick your toe in the pond.

Tip # 23 – Do not limit your sourcing. I, for one, have had tremendous success with flea markets. To the average person, they are just a mess. Look at them as a large thrift store. You have to dig through the jungle to find the gold. The difference between a flea market and a thrift store is often times that nugget of gold can lead to a large vein back at the sellers' storage locker. Build relationships.

Tip # 24 – Storage auctions. The television shows have really hurt this aspect of our business, but deals do still come up. If you do not want to attend these items, you may want to pass your business card out at some so others know what you are looking for. Of all the people I met at storage auctions, none of them were selling on Amazon. Most are looking for furniture, antiques, collectibles, and gold and silver. If they come across a cache of books, magazines, toys, and other items, they are most likely to take them to an auction where they will sell for pennies on the dollar.

Tip # 25 – Return to the scene of the crime... Just because Ross Dress for Less or Big Lots didn't have anything this week, it doesn't mean they won't next week. Talk to store personnel, and ask when they get their trucks in. First and foremost, remember to share the wealth -- build and foster relationships and above all, Be There!

Ok that is 25 tips, I could probably expound on another hundred or so but I will close with this one.

Tip # 1- Minus

Be careful paying people in advance. Along with my new found success, I found myself wanting to help others. As a result, on six different occasions I have fronted past business associates with money or product in exchange for them selling the items for me and sharing the profits. I have been burned six straight times. What started out with me being a blessing has turned into me being viewed, instead, as a burden. As a result, I anticipate writing off in excess of $14,000 from people I thought were my friends. If you don't have this problem, good for you; it is my Achilles' heel.

APPENDIX 2 – BUSINESS ANALYSIS OF FIRST 18 MONTHS

Total Cost of Goods (COG)	$465,826.00
Total Sales	$1,057,118.58
Total Items Sold	43,409
Average Selling Price	$24.35
Average Purchase Price	$9.34
Total Amazon Fees, including shipping	$321,136.48
Inbound shipping costs, estimated	$18,068.00
Mileage and miscellaneous	$12,685.00
Net profit not including mileage	$239,403.10
Return on Investment (ROI)	51.4%
Average Buy Box %	8.68%
Average refund rate	2.3%
Flea Markets sourcing	64.6%
Retail Arbitrage	35.4%
Health and Beauty	41.3%
Personal Care	30.9%
Toys, Games, Video Games	18.7%
Grocery	5.4%
Miscellaneous	3.7%

APPENDIX 3 – RECOMMENDED READING

Arbitrage By Chris Green

The authoritative guide on how it works, why it works, and how to make it work for you. This is basically the book that got me started. It is considered the bible in this industry, and Chris himself is a worthy shepherd of us, his flock.

Make Thousands on Amazon in 10 hours a Week By Cynthia Stine

How she turned $200 into $40,000 Gross Sales her first year in part-time online sales. This was the second book I read immediately after *Retail Arbitrage,* and it outlined the exact methodology for listing items on Amazon. Cynthia has her own website, blog, newsletter, and hands-on courses that she offers. Check her out.

Beat the Rush By Maureen Benner

5 Ways a new Online Marketplace Seller Can Prepare for Quarter Four and the Holidays. I just purchased this book in October and immediately regretted not purchasing it sooner. She offers sage advice for preparing for the Q4 phenomenon. I intended to read it again this week.

Note: There are many more books out there on selling on Amazon and eBay's platforms, and I have read many. Every book I have ever read has given me some knowledge, some tidbit of information, that has made it worth its purchase. I recommend you read as many as your time allows.

APPENDIX 4 – RECOMMENDED ONLINE SOURCES

Scanpower.com – https://unity.scanpower.com/
The most complete array of tools for scanning, listing, and repricing available on the internet.

Scanpower Facebook Group - https://www.facebook.com/groups/scanpower/
The quintessential Facebook group on doing FBA. Ask and you shall receive on this forum.

Scanner Monkeys Facebook Group
https://www.facebook.com/groups/scannermonkey/
A paid forum well worth the admission, for daily BOLOS and advice from other Scanner Monkeys. This is where I spend the majority of my time on Facebook, learning from the best.

Fast Turn Coaching- Facebook Group
https://www.facebook.com/groups/DuaneMalekCoaching/
Another paid forum featuring Fast Turn Radio guru Duane Malek. Duane answers questions on this group and provides instructional videos on doing FBA. I strongly recommend you subscribe if you are new to FBA.

Spreecasts by the following people:
Chris Green
Jay Bayne
Duane Malek
Andy Slammans

JOHN GROLEAU

Made in the USA
Lexington, KY
22 February 2014